Shape Stories

Six shape story patterns are featured in this section of *Creative Writing Ideas*. Use the questions below to stimulate prewriting discussions. Brainstorm to expand the word banks given on each form.

You can reproduce multiple pages for students who are ready to write longer stories, or use the worksheets as a template to cut writing paper.

Make individual or class books. Create a cover by tracing the shape onto construction paper.

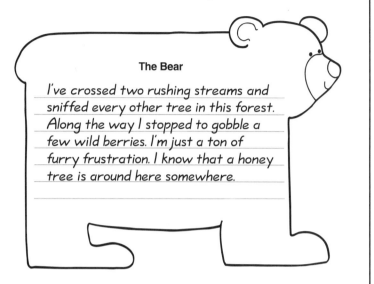

The Bear

I've crossed two rushing streams and sniffed every other tree in this forest. Along the way I stopped to gobble a few wild berries. I'm just a ton of furry frustration. I know that a honey tree is around here somewhere.

The Bear - Page 2
Think about this:
1. Describe how I look.
2. Where can you find me?
3. Name some foods I like.
4. What can I do?

The Planet - Page 3
Think about this:
1. What is the name of this planet?
2. What is the weather like?
3. What grows here?
4. Are there any animals on this planet?
5. What can happen on this planet?

The Whale - Page 4
Think about this:
1. Describe my size, shape, and color.
2. What else is special about how I look?
3. In what kinds of places can you find me?
4. How many kinds of whales do you know about?

The Spaceship - Page 5
Think about this:
1. What shape am I?
2. What am I made of?
3. What would you need to take to travel in me?
4. Where can I go?

The Elephant - Page 6
Think about this:
1. What do I look like?
2. Where do I live?
3. What kinds of food do I eat?
4. What are some of the things I can do?

The Shoe - Page 7
Think about this:
1. What does your shoe look like?
2. What is it made of?
3. Where did it come from?
4. What can you do wearing this shoe?

The Bear

Word Bank

climb	claw	wild
stream	awkward	honey
forest	furry	berries

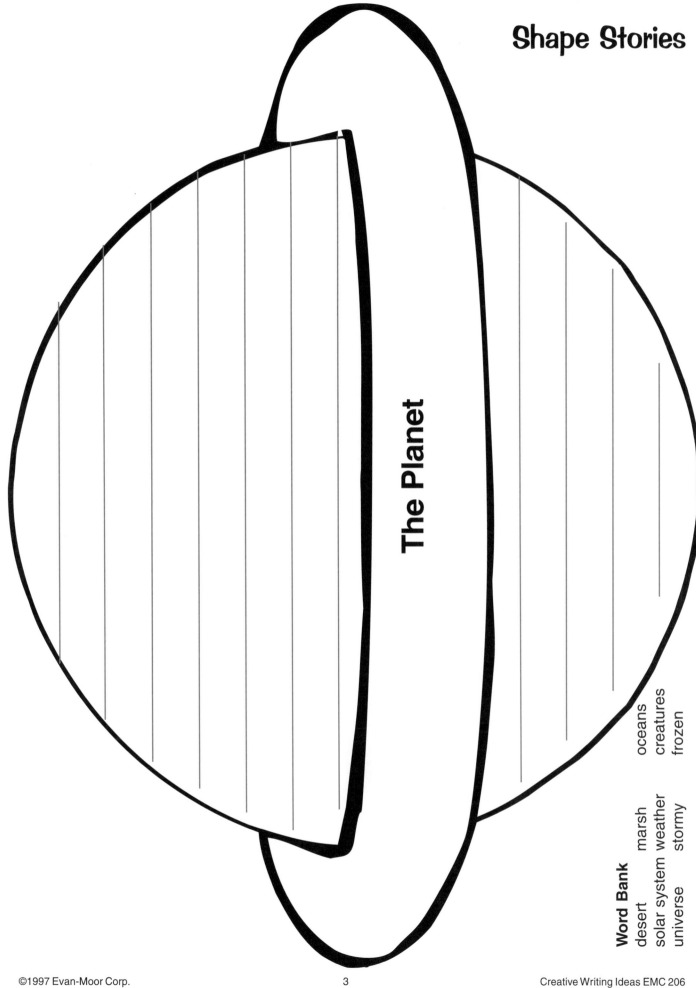

The Planet

Word Bank
desert   marsh
solar system   weather   oceans
universe   stormy   creatures
frozen

The Whale

Word Bank

gigantic	immense	dive	migrate	blubber
ocean	breathe	baleen	blow hole	mammal

Creative Writing Ideas EMC 206

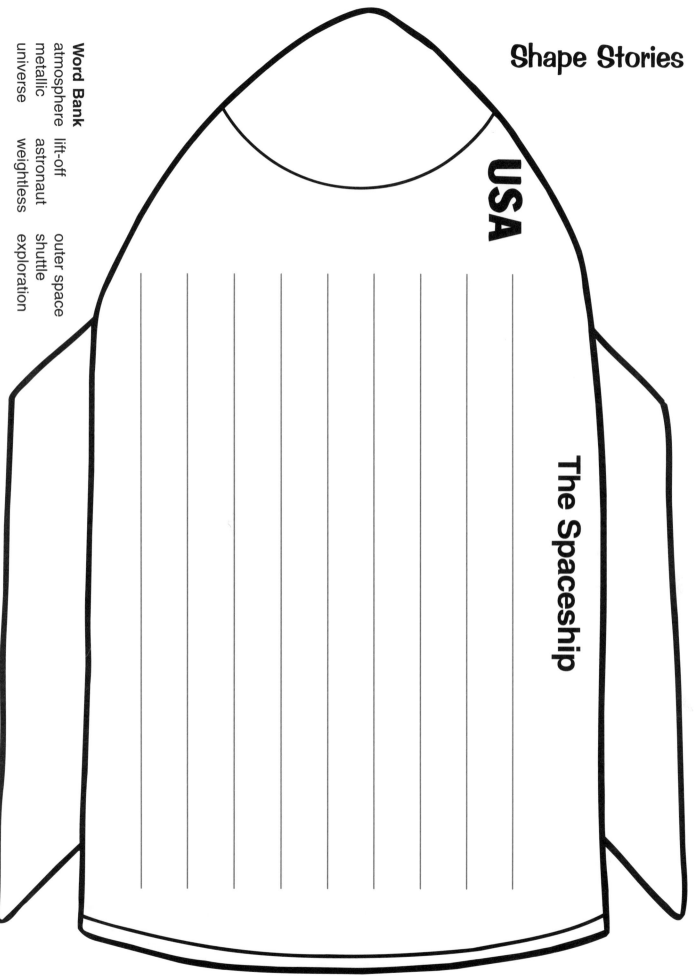

Shape Stories

USA

The Spaceship

The Elephant

Word Bank

wrinkled	heavy	tusks
huge	floppy	rough
Africa	India	jungle

Shape Stories

Word Bank

canvas	leather	laces
sole	heel	tread
toe	plastic	bounce

The Shoe

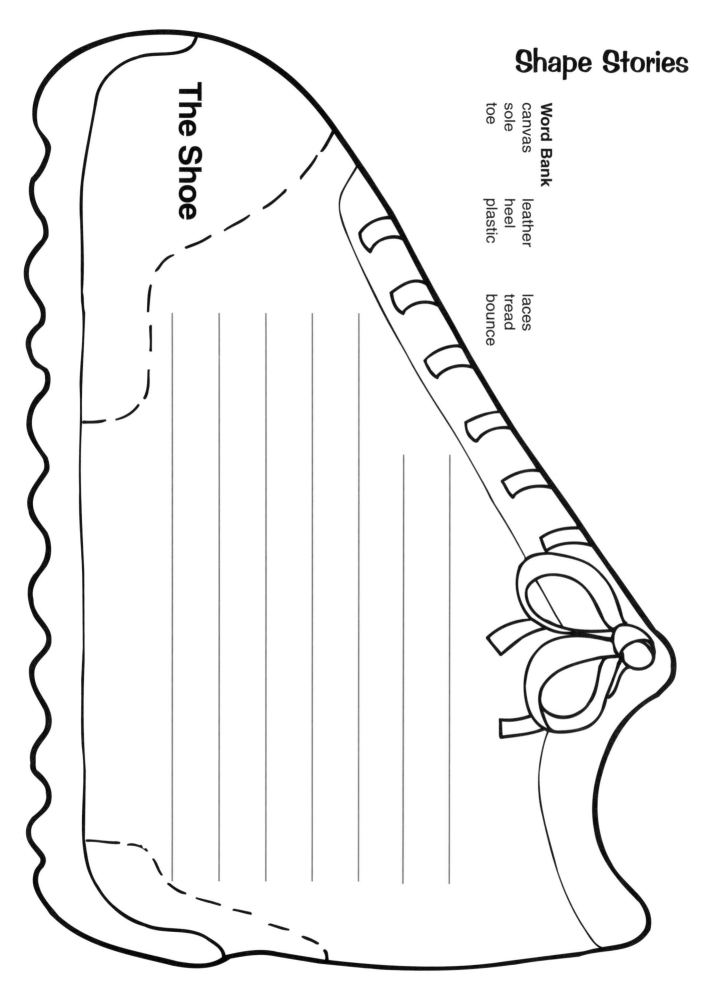

Draw and Write

This section of *Creative Writing Ideas* provides three lessons where the student will follow drawing steps and answer questions about the drawing. This is designed to stimulate imagination and to serve as a springboard to writing a story.

1. The student follows steps to complete a drawing. Add background details to the drawing to make it more interesting.

2. Answer the questions at the bottom of the page as a first step in writing the story. This beginning step will start the student thinking about the basic plot of the story.

3. Next the student uses the previous step to create a short story about the drawing. Depending on the writing level of the students, these stories cna range from simple to complex.

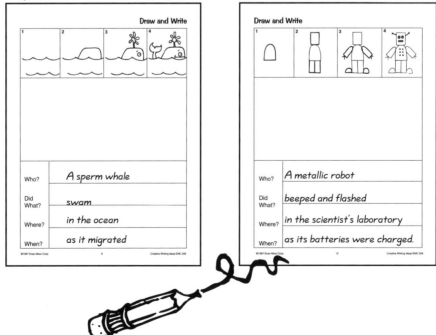

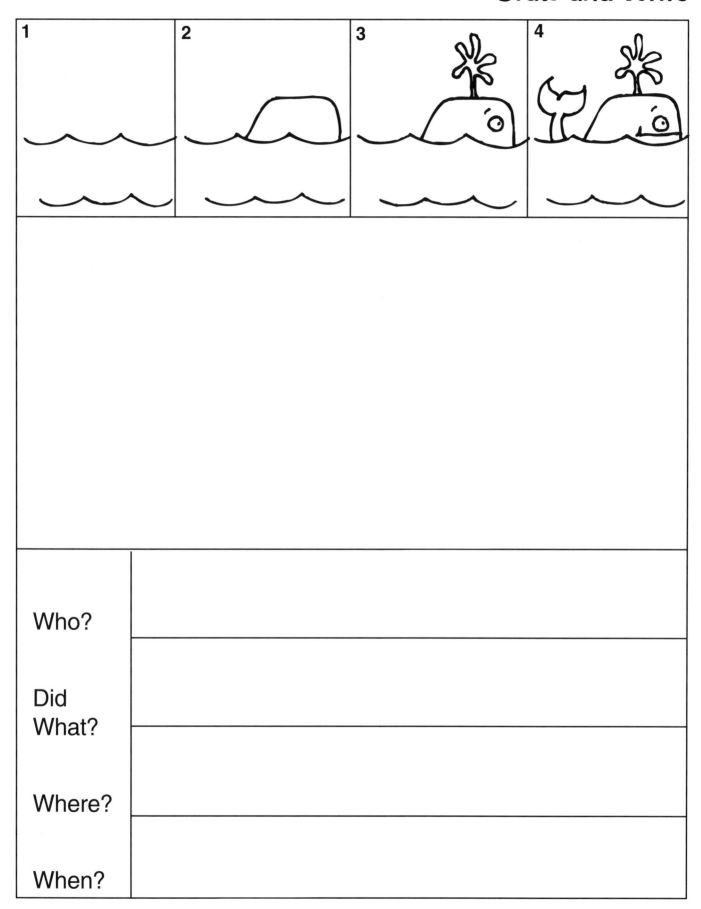

Who?

Did
What?

Where?

When?

Draw and Write

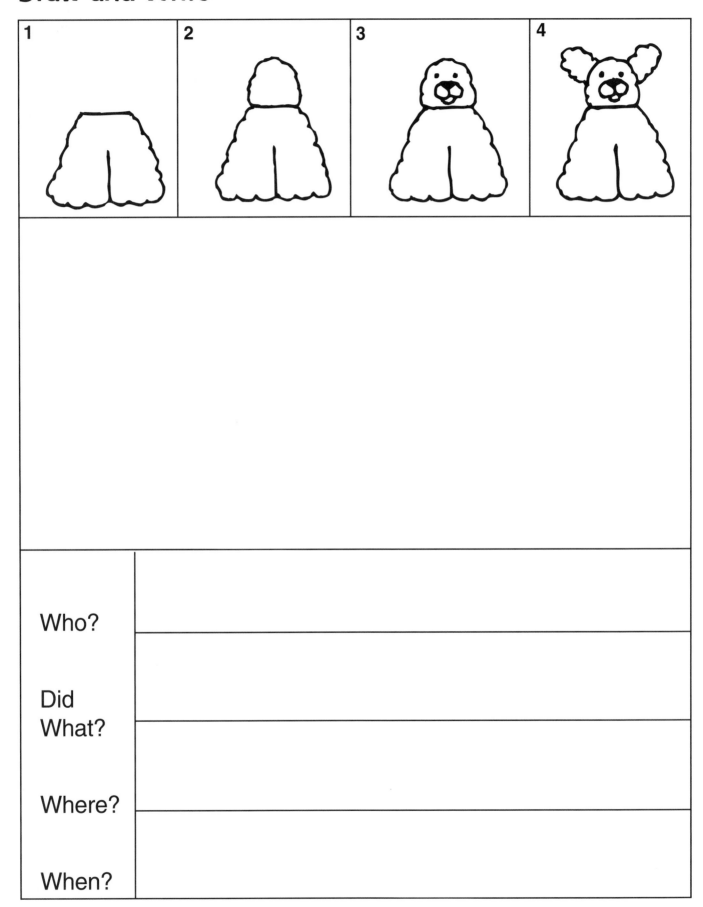

Who?	
Did What?	
Where?	
When?	

Who?

Did
What?

Where?

When?

Draw and Write

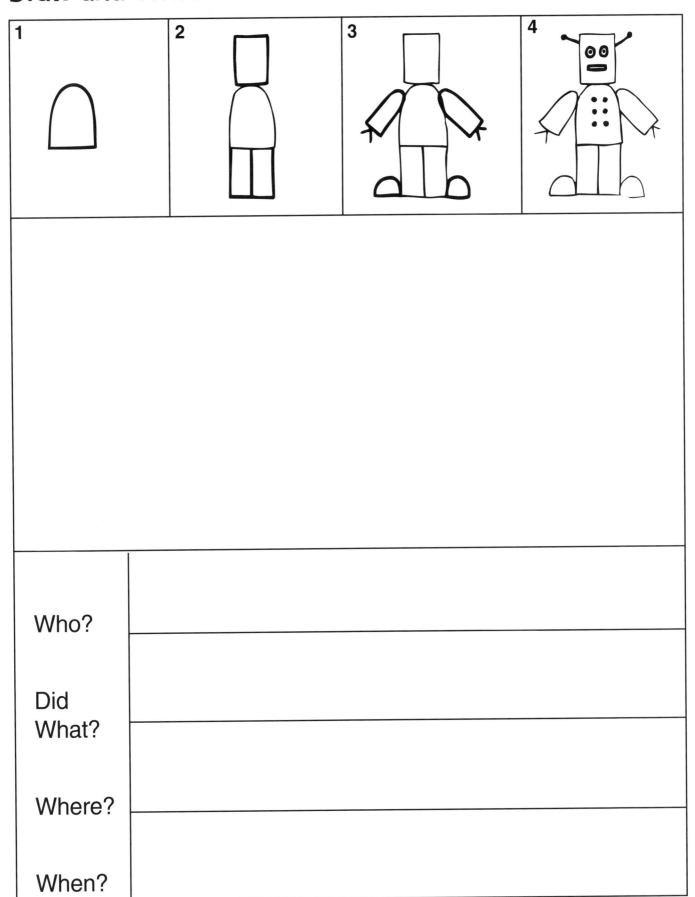

Who?	
Did What?	
Where?	
When?	

Riddles

In this section, students will participate in four fun riddle writing activities. Prepare for each riddle writing experience by asking questions that will stimulate the writing process.

Brown Bag Riddles — Page 14
- What is its size?
- What is its shape?
- What color is it?
- What is it made of?
- Where might you find it?

In My Lunch Box— Page 15
- What does it look like?
- How does it taste?
- How does it smell?
- When do you usually eat it?

Animal Pop-Ups— Page 16
- What is its physical appearance?
- Where does it live?
- What does it eat?
- What can it do?
- Does it make a sound?
- Do humans use it in any way?

Can You Guess Who I Am?— Page 17
- How does this person look?
- Describe the behavior of this person or tell an activity he/she can do.
- What is unique about this person?
- When and where did this person live?

Write about:

yourself	character from a story
classmates	someone from history
someone in your family	sports figure
someone from the movies or TV	teacher

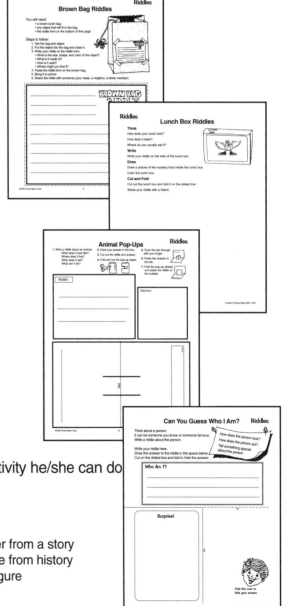

Riddles

Brown Bag Riddles

You will need:
- • a brown lunch bag
- • any object that will fit in the bag
- • the riddle form on the bottom of this page

Steps to follow:
1. Get the bag and object.
2. Put the object into the bag and close it.
3. Write your riddle on the riddle form.
   - • What is the size, shape, and color of the object?
   - • What is it made of?
   - • How is it used?
   - • Where might you find it?
4. Paste the riddle form on the brown bag.
5. Bring it to school.
6. Share the riddle with someone (your class, a neighbor, a family member).

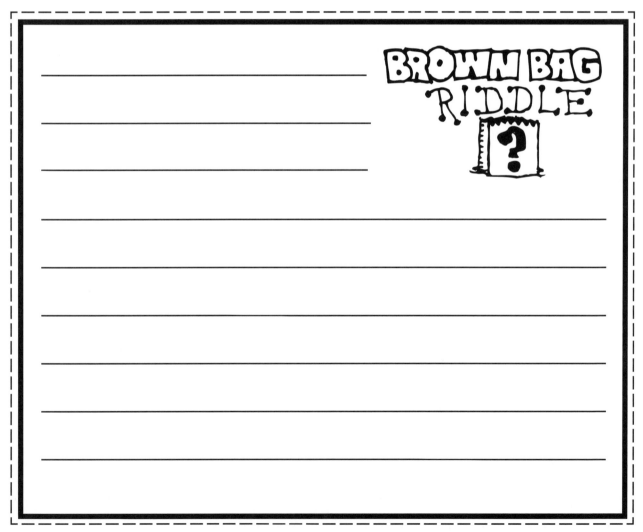

Lunch Box Riddles

fold

Think

How does your lunch look?

How does it taste?

Where do you usually eat it?

Write

Write your riddle on the side of the lunch box.

Cut and Fold

Cut out the lunch box and fold it on the line.

Draw

Draw a picture of the mystery food inside the lunch box.

Color the lunch box.

Share your riddle with a friend.

Write riddle here.

fold

Lunch Box Riddle

This belongs to:

Riddles

Animal Pop-Ups

1. Write a riddle about an animal.
   - What does it look like?
   - Where does it live?
   - What does it eat?
   - What can it do?

2. Draw your answer in the box.
3. Cut out the riddle and answer.
4. Cut out and fold the pop-up form. Fold and cut the pop-up tab.

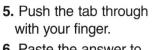

5. Push the tab through with your finger.
6. Paste the answer to the tab.
7. Fold the pop-up closed and paste the riddle on the outside.

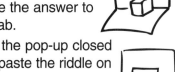

Riddle:

_____

_____

_____

_____

Answer:

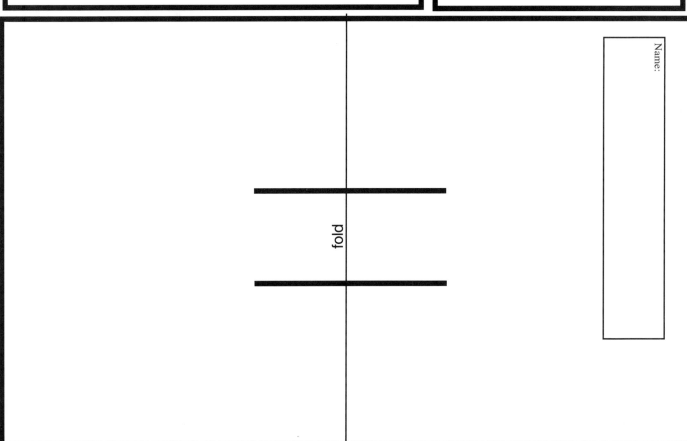

fold

Name:

Can You Guess Who I Am?

Riddles

Think about a person.
It can be someone you know or someone famous.
Write a riddle about the person.

Write your riddle.
Draw the answer to the riddle in the space below.
Cut on the dotted line and fold to hide the answer.

How does the person look?
How does the person act?
Tell something special about the person.

Riddle:

Who Am I?

_____

_____

_____

cut

Surprise!

fold

Fold this over to hide your answer.

 Creative Writing Ideas EMC 206

Sequence and Write

In this section of *Creative Writing Ideas,* students put pictures in the correct order and then write a paragraph about each picture to create a complete story.

Students will cut the pictures apart and lay them in the boxes in sequential order. Make sure the sequence makes sense before gluing the pictures in place.

Now write about each picture. These exercises help students to tell a story in a sensible order. For older students, the pictures aid in learning when to start a new paragraph because a new idea is being described.

The Boat - Page 19

An Adventure - Page 22

Cat and Bird - Page 25

Super Boy - Page 28

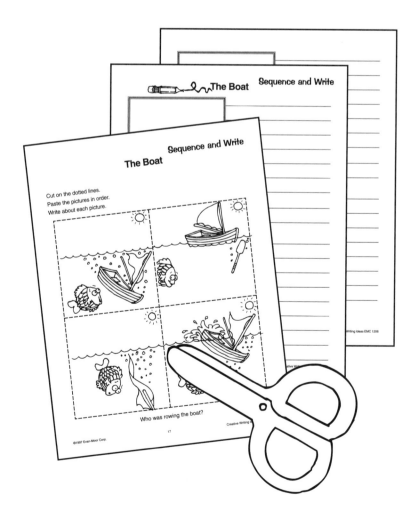

The Boat

Cut on the dotted lines.

Paste the pictures in order.

Write about each picture.

Who was rowing the boat?

Sequence and Write

The Boat

Creative Writing Ideas EMC 206

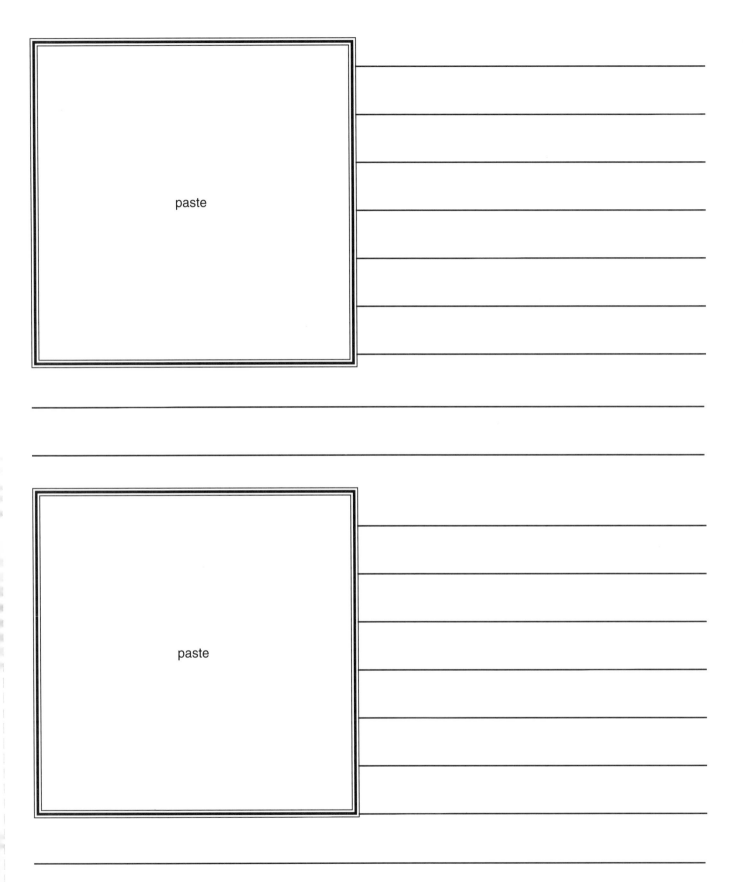

paste

paste

The End

Sequence and Write
An Adventure

Cut on the dotted lines.

Paste the pictures in order.

Write about each picture.

Where will he travel in this balloon?

An Adventure

paste

_____
_____
_____
_____
_____
_____
_____

_____

_____

paste

_____
_____
_____
_____
_____
_____

_____

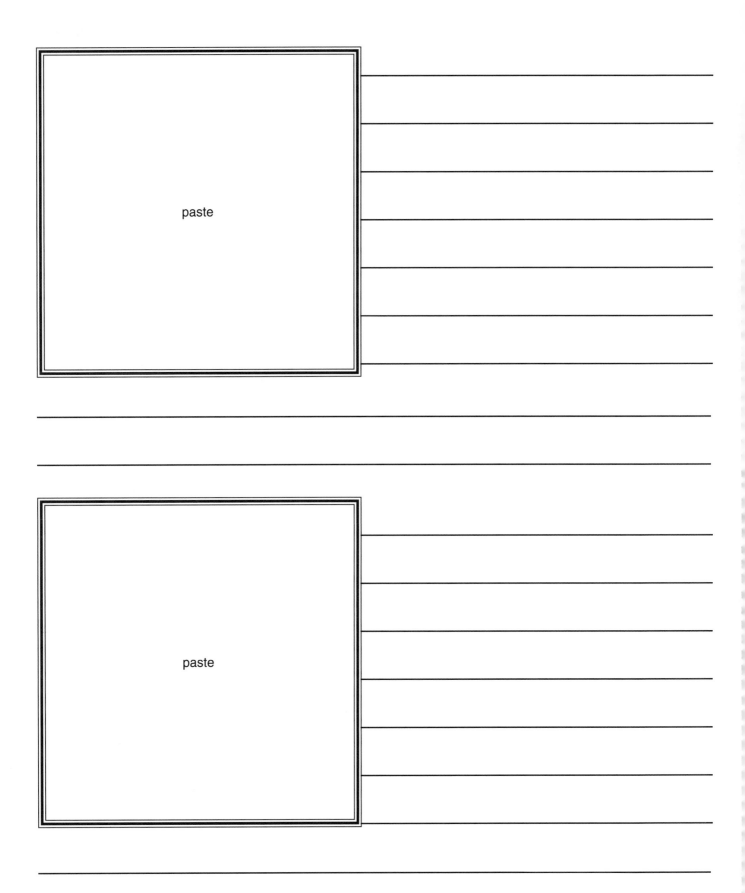

The End

Cat and Bird

Cut on the dotted lines.

Paste the pictures in order.

Write about each picture.

Will the cat try to catch that bird again?

Sequence and Write

Cat and Bird

paste	_____

paste	_____

paste	_____

paste

_____
_____
_____
_____

paste

_____
_____
_____
_____

paste

_____
_____
_____
_____

The End

Sequence and Write

Super Boy

Cut on the dotted lines.

Paste the pictures in order.

Write about each picture.

Will the cat try to catch that bird again?

paste

_____
_____
_____
_____
_____

paste

_____
_____
_____
_____

paste

_____
_____
_____
_____

paste	
paste	
paste	

The End

Fill in the Missing Words

Descriptive adjectives and verbs make writing so much more interesting to read. Which of the sentences below creates a more vivid picture in the reader's mind?

The cat went after the bird.

The stealthy, gray cat slinked noiselessly through the weeds toward the unsuspecting bird.

The four activities in this section of *Creative Writing Ideas* provide practice in using descriptive adjectives and verbs.

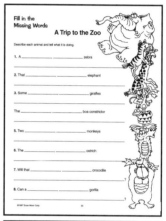

A Trip to the Zoo - Page 32
Students will practice using adjectives and verbs in this activity. Select two words to describe the animal named; then tell what the animal is doing.

A *tall, spotted* giraffe *nibbled leaves from a tree.*
That *small, angry* monkey *chattered loudly.*

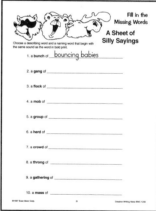

A Sheet of Silly Sayings - Page 33
Here's a really entertaining way to practice adjectives and nouns. Provide one adjective and one noun that begin with the same letter or sound as the "group" word given.

a bunch of *busy boys*
a bunch of *barefoot boxers*
a bunch of *beautiful blossoms*

The Race - Page 34
Beth and Tabby - Page 35
A short story is provided. Students fill in the blanks by choosing words from the Work Bank provided at the bottom of the page. The adventurous may wish to make up their own answers.

Creative Writing Ideas EMC 206

Fill in the
Missing Words

A Trip to the Zoo

Describe each animal and tell what it is doing.

1. A _____, _____ zebra

_____

2. That _____, _____ elephant

_____

3. Some _____, _____ giraffes

_____

The _____, _____ boa constrictor

_____

5. Two _____, _____ monkeys

_____

6. The _____, _____ ostrich

_____

7. Will that _____, _____ crocodile

_____ ?

8. Can a _____, _____ gorilla

_____ ?

32

A Sheet of Silly Sayings

Choose a describing word and a naming word that begin with the same sound as the word in bold print.

1. a **bunch** of _bouncing babies_

2. a **gang** of _____

3. a **flock** of _____

4. a **mob** of _____

5. a **group** of _____

6. a **herd** of _____

7. a **crowd** of _____

8. a **throng** of _____

9. a **gathering** of _____

10. a **mass** of _____

Fill in the
Missing Words

The Race

Fill in the blanks to create an exciting story about race cars.

BANG! went the starting gun. The _____race had begun.

_____ went the motors of the _____,

_____ racing cars. Number 7 _____ around a

_____curve. Down the _____track

_____ the cars. Number 19 was ready to pass when

_____ his tire went flat! Too bad Number 19! Number 7

_____ over the finish line to win the _____race.

_____went the crowd. Number 7 felt very _____.

Number 19 went_____ back to the pit. Maybe next time he would

be the winner.

Word Box

Use these words or make up answers of your own.

exciting	dusty	smooth	chug-chug
powerful	sped	slowly	muddy
roared	proud	thrilling	zoomed
sadly	shiny	hurrah	plop
hiss	flat	hummm	tired
championship	hurried	suddenly	dangerous
slick	steep	excited	

Beth and Tabby

This story is missing all the sound words.
Fill in the blanks to create an exciting story about Beth and Tabby.

_____ went the alarm clock. Beth leaped out of bed.

_____ went her blankets onto the floor. _____went her

feet. She heard a _____, _____, _____

sound outside. Her bedroom slippers went_____as she hurried to the

window. Hailstones were _____ all around. _____,

_____ went the chunks of ice on the roofs of cars and houses.

_____! _____! _____!There

was a noise at the back door. Poor Tabby had been left outside. Beth hurried to let her

cat in. As Beth slammed the door with a _____, Tabby jumped up and

began licking her face. _____!

Word Box

Use these words or make up answers of your own. You may add endings to these words. Use a
word more than once if you wish.

bang	meow	gurgle	plop	tick-tock	buzz
crash	flip-flop	blub-blub	splat	slurp	scratch
slunk	creak	purr	hiss	swish	boom
pow	click	rattle	crunch	hum	pitter-pat

Story Starters

Sometimes the hardest part of writing a story is getting those first few words down. Story starters give students a place to begin thinking and writing.

Eleven interesting story starters complete with illustration and writing lines are provided in this section of *Creative Writing Ideas*.

How to Get Started

Help your students get revved up to write by talking about each story starter.

- What are all the possibilities you can think of?
- What choices does the character have?
- What would happen if the character did _____?
- How will the story end?

Help writers to clarify their stories by telling some stories orally before beginning to write.

Make a list of words and phrases that might be useful in the story.

Story Starters

Read the story starter. Think about what will happen next. Use your fantastic imagination to finish the story.

Carmen and her dad went fishing at the lake. Dad caught several fish, but when Carmen pulled in her hook and line she found...

_____

_____

_____

_____

_____

_____

_____

_____

Story Starters

Read the story starter. Think about what will happen next. Use your fantastic imagination to finish the story.

Aunt Ethel sent George a plant for his birthday. George woke up in the middle of the night and heard the plant say...

_____

_____

_____

_____

_____

_____

_____

_____

_____

Story Starters

Read the story starter. Think about what will happen next. Use your fantastic imagination to finish the story.

Sean had come up with a clever plan to find the treasure hidden by the leprechaun in the woods behind his house.

_____

_____

_____

_____

_____

_____

_____

_____

_____

Story Starters

Read the story starter. Think about what will happen next. Use your fantastic imagination to finish the story.

As they explored the bottom of the deep cave, the team of scientists were surprised to find...

_____

_____

_____

_____

_____

_____

_____

_____

_____

Read the story starter. Think about what will happen next. Use your fantastic imagination to finish the story.

Alex climbed into his time machine, set the dial, and pushed the start button. Woosh! Off Alex went to explore Earth in the year...

_____

_____

_____

_____

_____

_____

_____

_____

Story Starters

Read the story starter. Think about what will happen next. Use your fantastic imagination to finish the story.

A small brown bunny peeked out of his burrow one summer afternoon. The bunny was feeling very hungry, but there was a fox sitting nearby. "How can I get by that fox?" he wondered.

_____

_____

_____

_____

_____

_____

_____

_____

_____

_____

Story Starters

Read the story starter. Think about what will happen next. Use your fantastic imagination to finish the story.

"Uh, oh! My pick-up truck has broken down. What do I do now?" The farmer didn't know that strange help was just over the hill coming his way.

_____

_____

_____

_____

_____

_____

_____

_____

Story Starters

Read the story starter. Think about what will happen next. Use your fantastic imagination to finish the story.

    It was a dark, cold morning. It had been snowing since late last night. When Sal walked out the front door, he saw something unusual.

_____

_____

_____

_____

_____

_____

_____

_____

_____

Story Starters

Read the story starter. Think about what will happen next. Use your fantastic imagination to finish the story.

Mother's Day was almost here. Jeri still needed money to buy her mother a gift. Mrs. Todwater hired her to walk her Great Dane. As Jeri started down the street with the huge dog…

_____

_____

_____

_____

_____

_____

_____

_____

_____

Story Starters

Read the story starter. Think about what will happen next. Use your fantastic imagination to finish the story.

Tasha was excited. Her parents said she could plan her birthday party all by herself. Tasha decided to …

_____

_____

_____

_____

_____

_____

_____

_____

_____

Read the story starter. Think about what will happen next. Use your fantastic imagination to finish the story.

The astronaut was driving across a wide crater when suddenly his lunar rover began to sink into the moon dust.

_____

_____

_____

_____

_____

_____

_____

_____

Cartoons

Kids love cartoons. In this section of *Creative Writing Ideas*, young writers are motivated to add their own words to four sets of cartoon pictures.

Use the discussion questions below as a part of your prewriting activities.

At the Pond - Page 49

- What could be happening at the pond?
- How would you describe each animal's expression?
- Why might each animal feel that way?
- What do you think each is saying?

The Runner - Page 50

- Why is this character running? (toward what? away from what?)
- How is the runner feeling?
- What might happen during the run?

Sweet Dreams - Page 51

- From the character's expression, what type of dream do you think is going on?
- What things might the character be dreaming?
- Is this a story with a beginning, a middle, and an end?
- Are the animals having the same dream?

Penguin Comics - Page 52

- What kinds of problems might penguins have?
- Think about how each penguin looks. What could be causing these expressions and actions?
- What could each penguin be saying?

Directions:
1. Follow the instructions on page 52 to make a cartoon story.
2. On page 53, complete the cover for your comic book.

       Creative Writing Ideas EMC 206

At the Pond

Fill in the bubbles.

 Creative Writing Ideas EMC 206

Cartoons

The Runner

Fill in the bubbles.

Sweet Dreams

What are you dreaming about?

_____

_____

_____

_____

_____

_____

_____

_____

_____

Cartoons

Penguin Comics

1. Color and cut.
2. Organize the pictures on pages 54 and 55 to tell a story.
3. Write in the speech bubbles.
4. Draw the background.

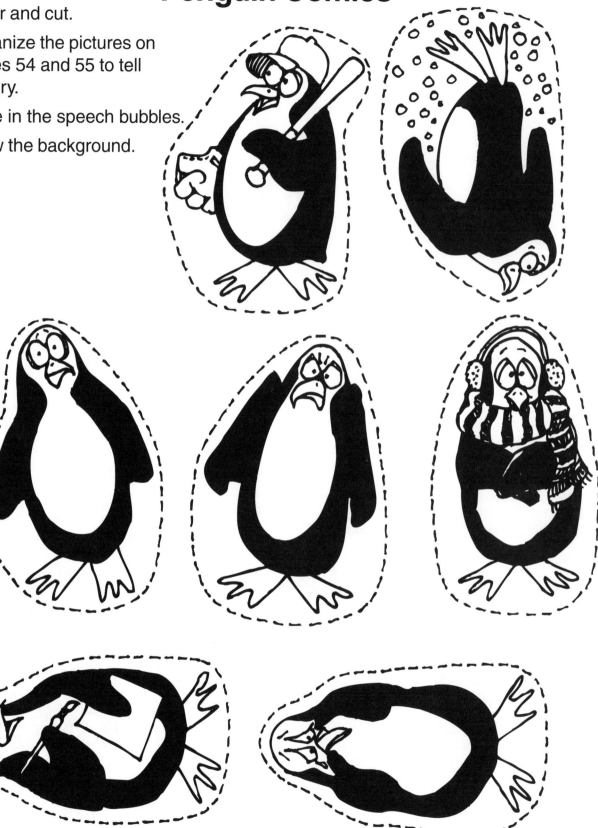

Creative Writing Ideas EMC 206

Penguin Comics

by:

Creative Writing Ideas EMC 206

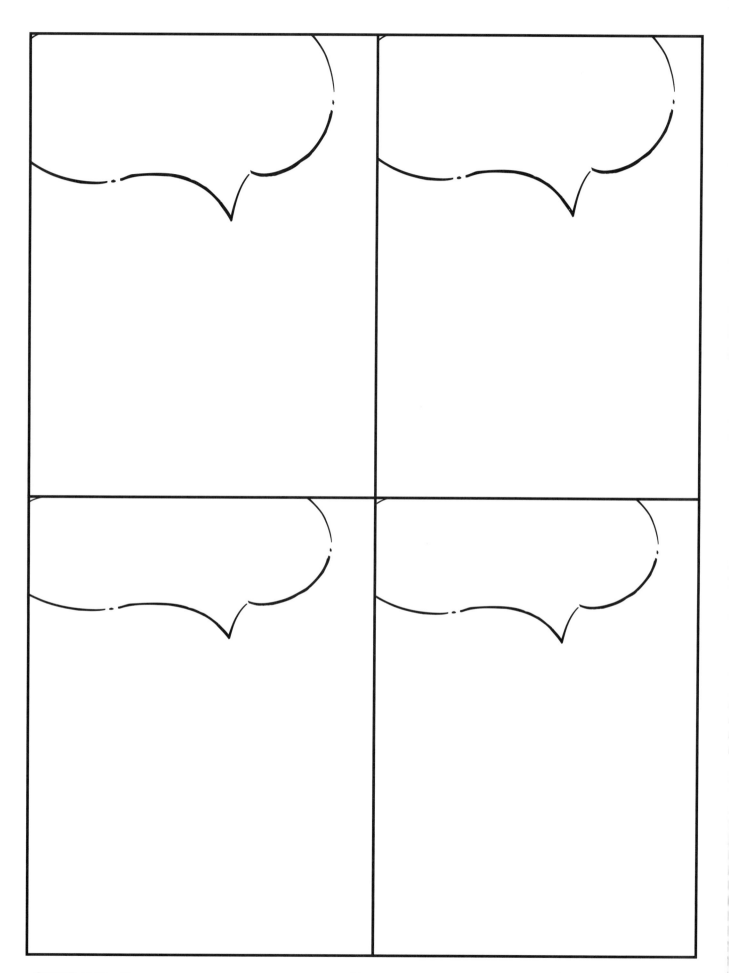

Creative Writing Ideas EMC 206

The End

 Creative Writing Ideas EMC 206

Descriptive Paragraphs

In this section of *Creative Writing Ideas*, students will have the opportunity to use good descriptive language to write about objects, feelings, and people. Help students get ready to write by discussing each topic using the questions provided below.

Describing Objects - Page 57
- What does the object look like? (color, size, shape, texture)
- What other characteristics does it have? (taste, smell, sound)
- How is it used?
- Where can you find it?

Describing Feelings - Page 63
- What are some of the feelings people experience?
  (happy, sad, disappointed, embarrassed, excited, fearful, etc.)
- What experiences can cause these feelings?
- Have you ever felt _____ ?
- What did you do?

Describing Places - Page 67-68
- Where is this place located?
- What are its physical characteristics?
  (how it looks, feels, smells, etc.)
- What is special or unusual about this place?

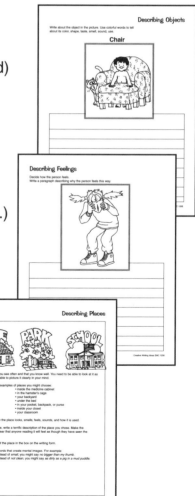

Describing Objects

Write about the object in the picture. Use colorful words to tell about its color, shape, taste, smell, sound, use.

Chair

Describing Objects

Write about the object in the picture. Use colorful words to tell about its color, shape, taste, smell, sound, use.

Kite

Describing Objects

Write about the object in the picture. Use colorful words to tell about its color, shape, taste, smell, sound, use.

Ice Cube

Describing Objects

Write about the object in the picture. Use colorful words to tell about its color, shape, taste, smell, sound, use.

Pie

Write about the object in the picture. Use colorful words to tell about its color, shape, taste, smell, sound, use.

Bubble

Describing Objects

Write about the object in the picture. Use colorful words to tell about its color, shape, taste, smell, sound, use.

The Bone

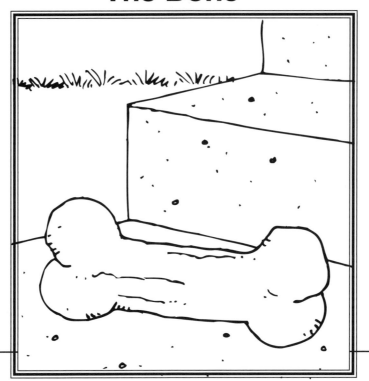

Describing Feelings

Decide how the person feels.
Write a paragraph describing why the person feels this way.

Describing Feelings

Decide how the person feels.
Write a paragraph describing why the person feels this way.

Describing Feelings

Pretend that this object has feelings.
Write a paragraph describing how it feels.

Describing Feelings

Pretend that this object has feelings.
Write a paragraph describing how it feels.

Describing Places

Select a place you see often and that you know well. You need to be able to look at it as you write or be able to picture it clearly in your mind.

Here are some examples of places you might choose:
- inside the medicine cabinet
- in the hamster's cage
- your backyard
- under the bed
- in your pocket, backpack, or purse
- inside your closet
- your classroom

Think about how the place looks, smells, feels, sounds, and how it is used.

On the next page, write a terrific description of the place you chose. Make the description so clear that anyone reading it will feel as though they have seen the place too.

Draw a picture of the place in the box on the writing form.

Hint: Think of words that create mental images. For example:
Instead of *small*, you might say *no bigger than my thumb.*
Instead of *not clean*, you might say *as dirty as a pig in a mud puddle.*

Describing Places

where:

descriptive words:

Writing Directions

Here's how to put on a coat...

Writing directions requires thinking clearly about the sequence in which something occurs. It also requires being thorough so that no steps or necessary parts are left out.

This section of *Creative Writing Ideas* provides ten opportunities to write clear, step-by-step directions.

As a prewriting experience, help students to tell the steps of a common activity, such as putting on a jacket, making a sandwich, wrapping a present, etc. It is especially helpful to do each step as you describe it. In that way, missing steps are easy to spot.

How to... Pages 70
The first five activities provide the opportunity to list the steps in doing an activity - either a common, everyday one (brushing teeth) or one requiring the use of imagination (capturing an elephant).

Very Unusual Recipes - Pages 76
Children love to create wild and wacky (and, yes, disgusting) combinations of ingredients. These two writing activities allow them to generate two very unusual recipes.

How to Get There - Pages 78
Giving directions from a starting point to a particular location is a valuable skill. The first writing experience requires looking at a map; the second necessitates being a keen observer of your surroundings.

How to...

Think about how you would do the activity below. Write detailed directions to tell how to do it. Don't leave out any steps!

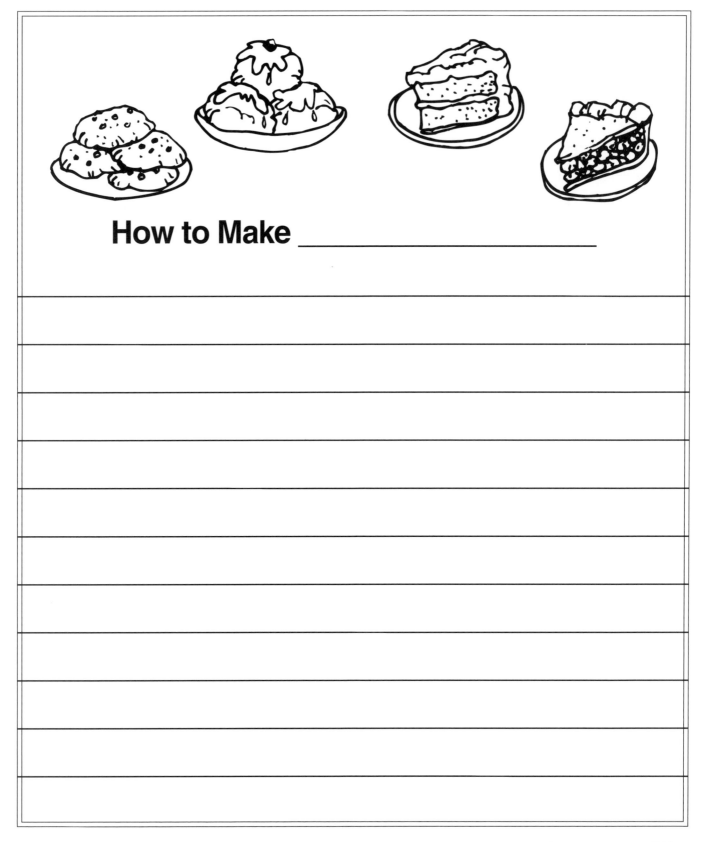

How to Make _____

Think about how you would do the activity below. Write detailed directions to tell how to do it. Don't leave out any steps!

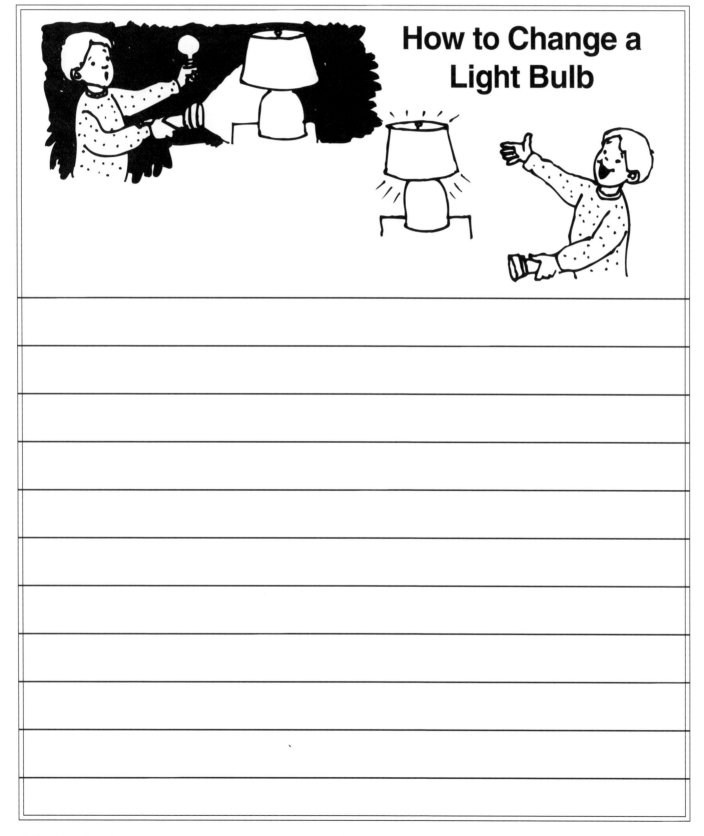

How to Change a Light Bulb

How to...

Think about how you would do the activity below. Write detailed directions to tell how to do it. Don't leave out any steps!

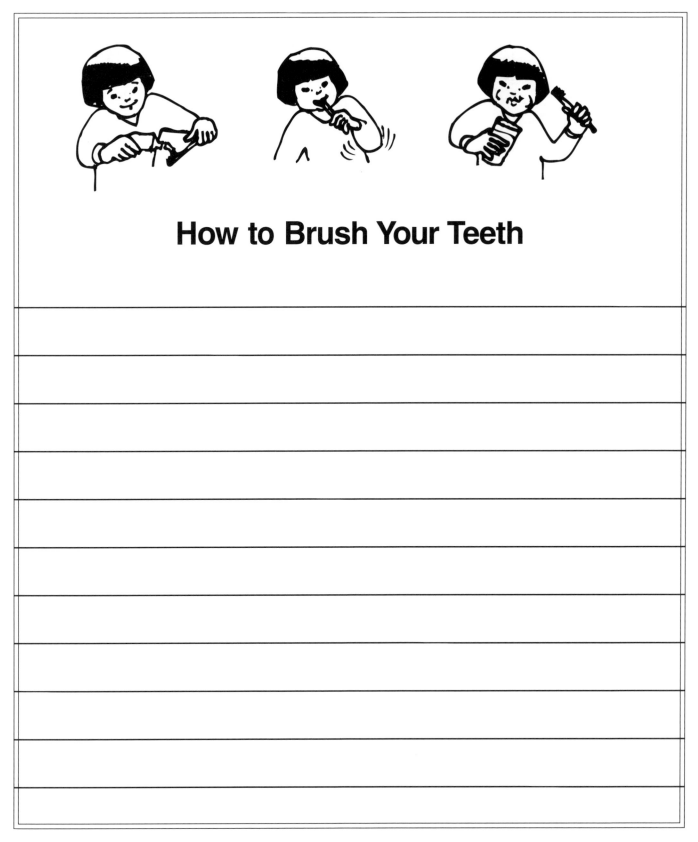

How to Brush Your Teeth

Think about how you would do the activity below. Write detailed directions to tell how to do it. Don't leave out any steps!

How to Get a Cat Off a Telephone Pole

How to...

Think about how you would do the activity below. Write detailed directions to tell how to do it. Don't leave out any steps!

How to Capture a Wild Elephant

Think about how you would do the activity below. Write detailed directions to tell how to do it. Don't leave out any steps!

How to Get Out of an Eight-Foot Hole

Very Unusual Recipes

Witch's Brew

What will you put in this brew?

_____   _____

_____   _____

_____   _____

Now how are you going to use this special brew?

_____

_____

_____

_____

_____

_____

_____

_____

Draw a picture showing how someone would look after using your Witch's Brew.

Super Stuff
The Drink of Champions

Ingredients:

_____

_____

_____

_____

_____

How to prepare "Super Stuff:"

_____

_____

_____

_____

_____

_____

_____

_____

start
here

Treasure Hunt

Study the treasure map.

Write out the directions for getting from the hut to the treasure chest.

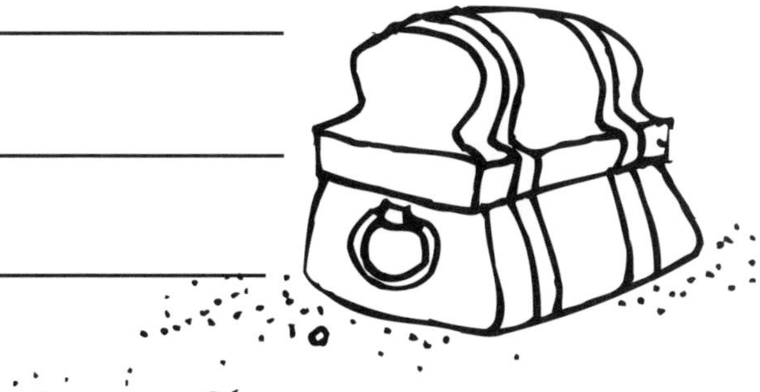

_____

_____

_____

_____

_____

_____

_____

_____

_____

_____

_____

How to Get There

From Here to There

Can you give clear directions to a new friend explaining how to get to your house? It is important to be very clear and to give the directions in the correct order so the other person does not get lost.

Choose one of the questions listed below. Think about the correct order for directions from one place to the other. Get a sheet of paper and write the directions carefully.

- How can someone go from the school to your backyard?
- How can you get from your desk to the pencil sharpener?
- How can you get from your classroom to the cafeteria?
- How do you get from your favorite park to the movie theater?
- How do you get from your kitchen at home to your bedroom?

How to Get There

From Here to There

Here's how to get from _____ to _____ .

Letter Writing

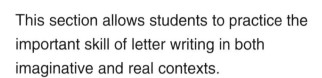

This section allows students to practice the important skill of letter writing in both imaginative and real contexts.

Page 83 shows the correct form for writing a friendly letter and for addressing the envelope. Make an overhead transparency or enlarge this page on a copier to create a chart. Discuss the information and encourage students to refer to it during the letter writing activities.

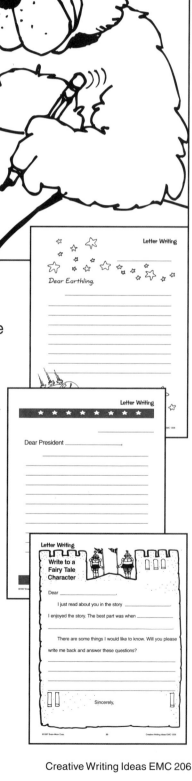

Alien Pen Pals! - Pages 84

Active imaginations can have free reign with this topic. The prewriting suggestions on page 84 will stimulate lots of ideas. Help students to be clear about the point of view used in the letter:

> "Remember, you are pretending to be the alien.
> The alien is writing a letter to **you**."

If students are enthused about this project, you might suggest that they write "back" to the "alien."

Dear Mr. President - Pages 86

Read and discuss the questions and reminders on page 86. Limit the questions and concerns to be included in the letter.

This activity provides an excellent opportunity to discuss the importance of neat handwriting and correct spelling and punctuation in clearly communicating one's ideas.

Be sure to actually mail the letter!

Write to a Fairy Tale Character - Page 88

Brainstorm a list of favorite fairy tales and the important characters in each. Let each student choose one character to be the recipient of the letter.

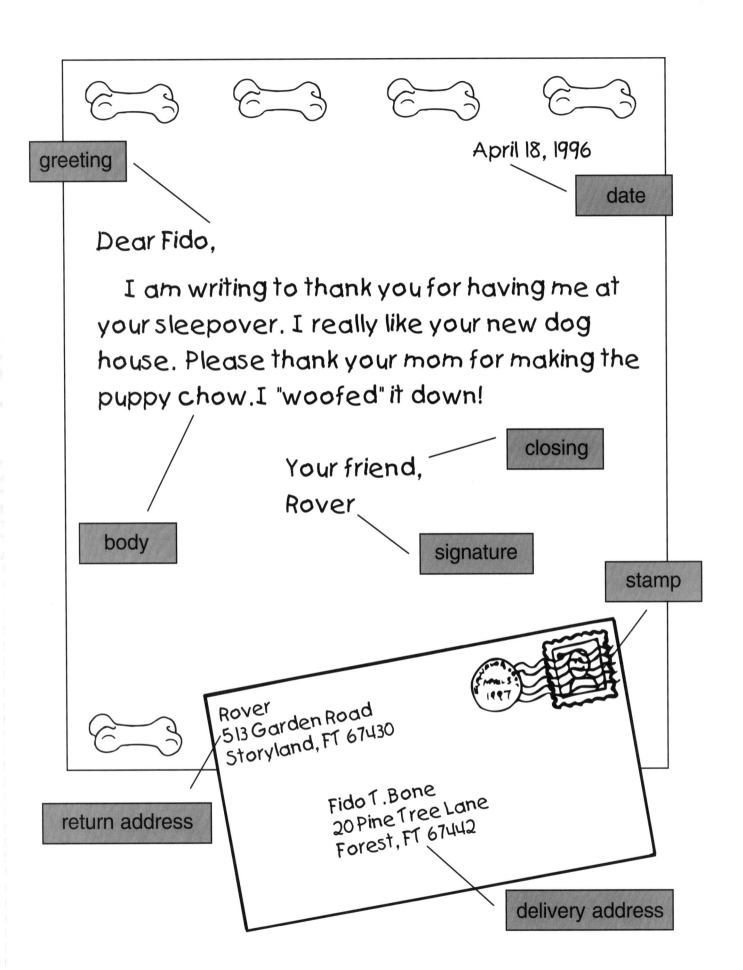

greeting

April 18, 1996

date

Dear Fido,

I am writing to thank you for having me at your sleepover. I really like your new dog house. Please thank your mom for making the puppy chow. I "woofed" it down!

closing

Your friend,
Rover

body

signature

stamp

Rover
513 Garden Road
Storyland, FT 67430

return address

Fido T. Bone
20 Pine Tree Lane
Forest, FT 67442

delivery address

Letter Writing

Alien Pen Pals

Turn your imagination to the stars. Is there anyone out there? Suppose one day you went to the mailbox and took out a letter from a far planet. What do you think the letter would say?

• Think about a name for your alien pen pal. Decide where this new friend lives. Decide what you think the letter might tell you about life on the alien planet. The letter might tell you:

    -what the strange pen pal looks like

    -what the planet looks like

    -all about his/her family

    -what kinds of pets they have

    -the games they play

    -their hobbies

• The letter might ask you:

    -What do you look like?

    -What does Earth look like?

    -Tell about your family.

    -What kinds of pets and games do Earthlings have?

• Now write the letter. Remember you are pretending to be the alien. Don't forget to include:

    -Date

    -Greeting

    -Body

    -Closing

    -Signature

_____

Dear Earthling,

_____

_____

_____

_____

_____

_____

_____

_____

_____ ,

_____

Letter Writing

Dear Mr. President

Here is your chance to let the President know how you feel.

Think about what you would like to say in your letter.

• Do you have a concern about something you want to tell him about?

• Is there something you think needs to be changed?

• Do you want to let him know you think he is doing a good job in some area?

• Do you want to ask him some questions about what being President is like?

• Do you want to ask anything about how you prepare for such a difficult position?

• Do you want to ask about his family?

• Do you want to know about his life when he was your age?

When you know what you are going to say to the President, write your letter on the writing form..

Use your best handwriting. Remember to include:

date	closing
greeting	signature
body	

Address your letter to:

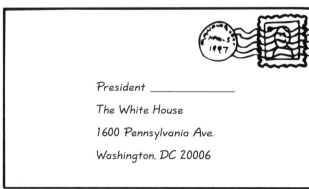

President _____

The White House

1600 Pennsylvania Ave.

Washington, DC 20006

_____

Dear President _____,

_____

_____

_____

_____

_____

_____

_____

_____

_____

_____ ,

_____

Letter Writing

Write to a Fairy Tale Character

Dear _____,

I just read about you in the story _____.

I enjoyed the story. The best part was when _____

_____.

There are some things I would like to know. Will you please

write me back and answer these questions?

_____

_____

_____

_____

Sincerely,

Poetry

It's true, poetry can be harder to write than prose, but some simple forms can be just as easy too. In this section, children get to try their hands at six poetry forms.

Cinquain Verse - Page 91

Cinquain verse does not rhyme. It follows a pattern of five lines and can be on any topic, frequently nature. The form presented here is simplified for use by children.

Line 1	One word *(title)*
Line 2	Two words *(describe the title)*
Line 3	Three words *(describe an action)*
Line 4	Four words *(describe a feeling about the subject)*
Line 5	One word *(refering back to the title)*

Here are two examples of cinquain verses written by children.

Owl	Otter
Swift, ferocious	Gentle baby
Watches for food	Dives for food
Soaring through the night	Loves the cool water
Hunter	Otter

The Name Game (Couplets) - Page 92

A couplet is two lines that rhyme. To create a name couplet:

1. Choose a name as the first line of the couplet.

2. Think of words that rhyme with the chosen name.

3. Make a sentence that ends with one of the rhyming words.

> Mrs. Anne Sneed
> Taught me to read.
>
> Jacques Cousteau
> Sails on Calypso.

Alphabet Poems (Acrostics) - Page 93

An acrostic is a sentence or phrase in which the words begin with the letters of a topic word.

1. Select a word.

2. List as many words as you can that describe or relate to the word.

3. Write the word vertically. Select one word from your list that starts with each letter of the word. Your goal is to create a descriptive phrase or sentence about the word.

d ashing
o ver
g round

l ovely
e ven
a fter
f alling

Shape Poems - Page 94

Finished shape poems are eye-catching displayed on a bulletin or usedas the cover for a report or a unit notebook.

Complete reproducible directions are given on page 94.

Haiku - Page 95

Haiku is a Japanese poetry form. It consists of three lines containing 17 syllables in this configuration:

LIne 1: *5 syllables*	*The hungry frog*	*Gentle raindrops fall.*
Line 2: *7 syllables*	*resting on a lily pad*	*Reflected in the puddles,*
Line 3: *5 syllables*	*dreams of careless flies.*	*thristy flowers drink.*

Traditional haiku usually refers to nature or the seasons.

Despite its lack of rhyme, haiku is difficult to write. Third graders and up can be successful with this form given ample modeling. Read samples of haiku to the class. Then write haiku poems together before assigning the writing as an independent activity.

Students should start with the thought and then "play" with the words to make the syllable count fit.

Limericks - Page 96

Limmericks follow an AABBA rhyming pattern. The meter is also specific. Exact meter should only be a factor with advanced groups. Read limericks (Edward Lear was a master) aloud so that students get a feel for the rhyme and meter.

It is helpful to begin by providing part of the rhyme and having the class provide the rest. For example:

> *There once was a kitten named Sam*
> *Who always was caught in a jam*
>
> _____
>
> _____
>
> *That mischevious kitten named Sam.*

A Cinquain

1. Choose a topic.
2. Write a cinquain.
3. Illustrate the poem.

Otter
Gentle baby
Dives for food
Loves the cool water
Otter

One Word
(title)

_____

Two Words
(describe title)

_____

Three Words
(describe an action)

_____

Four Words
(express a feeling)

_____

One Word
(refer back to title)

_____

Poetry

The Name Game

Mrs. Anne Sneed
Taught me to read.

Jacques Cousteau
Sails on Calypso.

1. Choose a name.
2. Make a list of words that rhyme with the name.
3. Write the verse.

_____

Line 1: Name

_____

Line 2: A rhyming sentence about the person.

_____

Line 1: Name

_____

Line 2: A rhyming sentence about the person.

Alphabet Poem

d ashing
o ver
g round

l ovely
e ven
a fter
f alling

1. Choose a word to be the topic of your poem.

2. Make a list of words that describe or relate to your word.

3. Write the topic word vertically in the narrow box. Pick words from the list that start with each letter in your word. Use them to make a sentence or phrase about the word.

Word List

Poetry

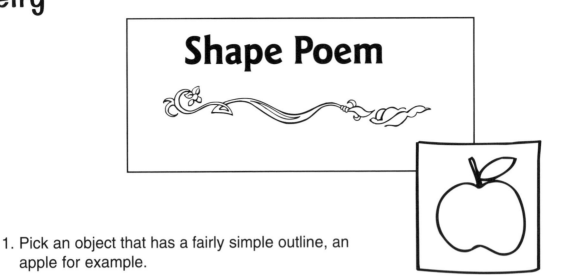

Shape Poem

1. Pick an object that has a fairly simple outline, an apple for example.

2. Draw the outline of your object using a dark crayon or marking pen.

3. Get a piece of writing paper. Make a list of words and phrases that describe the object.

   Arrange them in a way that sounds pleasing to you.

4. Paperclip a sheet of plain paper over your drawing. Write your description following the shape of the picture.

5. Mount your poem on a sheet of construction paper.

Creative Writing Ideas EMC 206

Haiku

Three lines containing 17 syllables which usually refer to nature or the season.

1. Choose a topic.
2. Write a haiku.
3. Illustrate your poem.

Line 1: *5 syllables* _____

_____

Line 2: *7 syllables* _____

_____

Line 3: *5 syllables* _____

_____

Creative Writing Ideas EMC 206

Poetry

Limericks

Remember:

• Lines 1 and 2 must rhyme.

• Lines 3 and 4 must rhyme.

• Line 5 refers back to line 1 and must rhyme with it.

There once was _____

That _____.

_____

_____

That _____.